Surfacing High on a New Wave of Poetry

BENNIE MIZELL DANIELS

PAGE PUBLISHING, INC.
New York, NY

First originally published by Page Publishing, Inc. 2017

ISBN 978-1-64027-122-7 (Paperback)
ISBN 978-1-64027-123-4 (Digital)

Printed in the United States of America

A Harbor
of Love Life
and Politics

Dedication to Dad

I wish to dedicate my first book to
my father of whom without his faith,
his belief in me, I would never have
developed such dedication and
determination toward my writing.
I recall the time that I wanted
his opinion about some of my poetry.
I wanted to know from him if it was
good enough to publish. As I began
reading (with mouth, song, and a Bible
in his hand)(a Dr. MLK. Jr. poem), he was so
elated, I thought he was having
a heart attack as he sucked in his breath
let it out and with that wide beautiful almost
toothless grin of his bellowed out, "What are
you waiting for? Let's get to smoking!"

Thank you, Dad!
(smile)
May you rest in peace!

Contents

Preface

a poetic buffet for people
with an insatiable appetite
for a delectable taste in poetry
as we venture into
the windows of
Ms. Bennie's world while
Riding high on
a new world of poetry

My Dad

(Deacon Benjamin F. Daniels)

My dad, my special dad,
a man who loved his guitar
and how he loved to play
sometimes at night
but mostly in the day
he loved children
especially his own
and for every generation
he provided a home
a man with a heart of gold
a loving mind and spirit
that never grew old
his smile was like a comforter
blanketing our every move
he provided us with wisdom
humor, transportation
and we were never out of food
he loved our mom
her name was Edith
he called her EO
and for all of these years
since God took her away
he never let her go
I am proud of my dad
just as proud as I can be
he's with her in heaven now
May they rest in peace.

Deacon Benjamin F. Daniels

The Breath Taker

With Mouth Song and a Bible in His Hand

Dr. Martin Luther King Jr.
A strong-minded courageous man who fought for equality
With mouth, song, and a Bible in his hand
Who brought the world together in a march for peace
When we thought prejudices against Blacks
Would never cease
Who said that freedom bells would ring
If everyone joined hands together and sing
("We shall overcome, we shall overcome")
Blows to the head! Blows to the gut!
They tried to stop him, but they couldn't shut him up
I had a dream, I've been to the mountaintop!
Let freedom bells ring! We could hear him shout
A man on a mission, absolutely no doubt
Martin Luther King Jr.
Put his life on the line, and he knew that pretty soon
It would be his time. He won the fight against segregation
And helped to bring peace throughout the nation
And with words of peace and Bible in hand
He made his way to the Promised Land

Original Stories
(In Poetic Form)

The Road to Happiness

(for husband and wife)

Wives cleave unto your husbands
Husbands cleave unto your wife
Make important decisions together
Make that a way of life
Be committed, thoughtful
Romantic and kind
And strengthen your love
With a Godly mind
Love your children
Love them with
Discipline and respect
And they will honor
And appreciate you
Even more in return
That's a choice
You won't regret
Do not let lust
Or let temptation
Lead you to sin
Control your thoughts
Don't let the devil in
Love honor and
Trust each other
And pray together each night
That you will be shown

Mercy and forgiveness
And be blessed with
The morning light
Follow the
Ten Commandments
And you'll have success
For in following
The word of God
Is a true road to happiness

Muhammad Ali!

(The Greatest!)

The man has guts, a fantastic poet
Blessed with stamina, wit, and grit
Stood up for his beliefs, to him
Here in America he wasn't free
The black and brown men had no
Justice had no Civil Rights, no equality
Here in the USA, his own home
Was stripped of his heavyweight title
He had given the world a fit and like
A golden gem, he mesmerized folks
With his rope a dope so beautiful to see
As he floated around his opponents
Stinging like a bee and the crowd hungry
For his boxing skills, shouting "Ali! Ali! Ali!"
The world's fastest and prettiest boxer
A powerful speaker a poet so show-biz-nee
With his Ali beat
Was stripped of his USA heavyweight crown
Suspended from boxing three years or more
For defending his religious belief
Was pushed off his throne
Regained it in Zaire
The people loved him there
And landed on his feet
Was world's greatest heavyweight
Champion at age twenty-three
Our hero, our Olympic and World's
Heavyweight Champion, our star
The great Muhammad Ali! Ali! Ali!

The Red Tails

(Tuskegee Airmen African American Heroes)

No finer men ever seen: even though their future
Only a field of shattering hopes and dreams
They broke the air force color barrier
They were a thousand strong
Ready and eager to get started
On a mission they made their own
To unite in protecting our white soldiers
And bringing our boys back home
They painted the end of their planes red
And were known as the Red Tails
And whenever they were on a mission
Their patriotism never failed
They bravely fought for America (Their own country)
Which treated them with bigotry and hate
Saw combat throughout the Mediterranean
North Africa and the European states
Escorted these aircrafts on missions
Protecting them from the enemy's fire
The Tuskegee Airmen didn't die in battle,
None became prisoners of war while
Saving the lives of other American soldiers
But nobody heard their cry
Such ungratefulness in some people and
Nobody knows why
With honor they did their duty
They had served their country well
They had their fellow soldiers back
Throughout a wall of hell

And saved them from countless attacks
They fought for them they protected them
But after risking their lives and returning home
Things were never good enough
They found that the war was still on
In America, in their own neighborhood
Some ungrateful citizen in the United States
Wouldn't let the prejudices cease so that
The Black soldiers could come home
To their wives and families and
Live in harmony and peace
There was prejudices against Afro Americans
That was never understood
After fighting for their country and returning
To the home they fought for, the home they loved
There was no justice and they weren't treated fair
Just soldiers in uniform and few seemed to care
Racism was rampant in America
Everywhere they could see
The enemy they had fought was welcomed
First-class citizens and
The Black man still wasn't free
The men in their infantry had fought many battles
But none like the ones they had at home
If they had not such strong Christian beliefs
And family unity, they would have felt all along
Then at last in year two thousand seven
Thanks to the former US President
G. W. Bush though long overdue but welcome
Who honored them with Congressional Medals,
For a job well done, and supplied them with
The recognition and appreciation they deserved

And returned them to their throne
Now the last three hundred out of a thousand
Black Tuskegee warriors can now smile
On their way to heaven and
The one's that's already gone can look down and see
At last that it was worth it to risk their lives
They have won their victory!

Our African Brother

(The Black Man)

One thing I can't understand
Why is there so much hatred
For the Black man
In the beginning
They were brought to America
In captivity as slaves
Under duress and oppressed
Worked hard and beaten too
Or nearly half to death
Their wives raped
Their children taken away
Their families torn apart
The Black Woman
Was as strong and as faithful
As allowed to be
Took white man's abuse
Yet raised her family
Stood side by side
With her man in the fields
Singing songs of encouragement
While the soils they tilled
Together they were instilled
With love and loyalty
Their only wish was to be free
And to escape
The bondage of slavery

Makeup of Our Destiny

The African was not born
A slave on their land
They were rich, proud, and free
Born as kings and queens
In their cultured world
They were people of royalty
Had no knowledge of other life
A cross the open sea
Had no knowledge of
The smoking gun
That brought them death despair
Oppression and into slavery
They were filled with song and rhythm
And instilled with the spirit to pray
Had no idea where they were headed
But knew they were on their way
Every nationality was brought here
On one kind of journey or another
For the family could not be complete
Without the African sister and brother
No! They were not born slaves on their land
But rich proud and free
Very essential to this journey
To complete the family
Racial prejudices are not acceptable
In the land of the free
And we must fight all injustices
For that is our destiny
Because in these United States
The land of the brave and home of the free
We will become the example of the world
For this is our destiny!

His Dream Lives On!

It was a rainbow coalition upon this land
When Dr. Martin Luther King Jr.
And thousands of people walked hand in hand
(Black, white, red, brown, and cream) A united team
Dr. King had a dream, a nonviolent peace plan
The reverends C. L. Franklin, Jessie Jackson, Al
Sharpton, and Ralph Albernathy and Harry Belafonte
And many others shared they all walked together
Proving how much they cared
Two women ignited the spark
A young girl name Claudette Colvin
And the gracious Ms. Rosa Parks both changed
History, both suffered the pain and went to jail
Like King did in his plan to prevail
Dr. King did not die in vain
He made his mark and staked his claim
Their visions were made a reality
When they won their fight for segregation to end
And although he's gone
His dream lives on for us and our liberty
or in his fight for justice and equality
He gave his life for you and me!

Smoking Joe, World Heavyweight Champion

(Joe Frazier, Most Exciting Opponent)

Hard-hitting Joe Frazier (Smoking Joe)
Had a mean punch
That would turn your lights out
He was one of the greatest boxers
Absolutely no doubt
(Not to leave George Foreman out)
Another world heavyweight champion
George was the biggest and the
Strongest but like Joe not the smartest
They were beaten by will and wit
Just one of Joe's punches
Would knock you to the floor
He didn't move too fast nor was he slow
He just kept closing in more, more, and more
Ali had a punch that would cut you deep
And as he used force
It would knock you off your feet
From the double-clutch shuffle and
The sting of the bee
Frazier had to keep moving to conquer Ali
Ali said, "Here I am come" and "Get me"
"I'll mess you up so bad, you won't be able to see"
Frazier was a great boxer but unlike Ali he was
Built broader and powerful, more like a freight train
Closing in, determined to get Ali, determined to win
Sometimes it seemed, they would take turns

Winning the world's heavyweight championship
They had both earned
The best fights in the world to see
Were the ones between the powerhouses
Mr. Joe Frazier!
and
Muhammad Ali!

Omali Yeshitela

(Joe Waller)

Omali Yeshitela
I acknowledge you to be
An honest brave and just man
A freedom fighter from a way back
While fighting to win our Civil Rights
Tore down the mural in
St. Petersburg City Hall
Degrading African Americans upon its walls
Exhibiting prejudices and disrespect
Shoving it in our face
So that we couldn't forget
One man stood up and fought for the right
To banish this mockery out of sight
Omali Yeshitela, we thank you!

Big T.

Big Tony C. really impresses me
With his Pandora's Box of talents
Will wonders never cease?
Just like Ali floats like a butterfly
On his rhythmic feet
He's a romanticist with stories to be told
And a huge amount of fortitude
Lady C. has groomed him well
A dynamic talent that really sells
With Robinson's studio performs as Act 3

The Jazz Man

(Alvin "Al" Downings)

Second to his children and Bunny (Bernice), his wife
To the great Al Downings, jazz was his life
Al Downings, a legend in Tampa Bay
Who brought the flavor of jazz to our fair cities
In his own special way the flavor of jazz in all its forms
Sweet swinging notes, spreading happiness and fun
Musically serenading his audiences while incorporating
The distinctive sound of jazz in each instrument to everyone
It started with young musicians and him not wanting them to
Perform in a bar especially for his daughter Evelyn
Who was his own favorite star
He sought a place of solace
Wherein families could feel safe and comfortable
While listening to the upbeat in the sound of jazz
Experiencing the knowledge of its presence and its past
while delving into the magic of its musical point of view
He sought a safe haven to present jazz to you
He began giving concerts on Sunday afternoons
To hear his group Allegro, no day was too soon
Ten years later Allegro was incorporated in Florida's state
Name changed to Al Downings Florida Jazz Association
Still has the same name up to this date
Each week they gave to you a different lesson featuring
different instruments that ended in a jam session
Starring individual instrumental soloist of the same kind
Playing his instrument blowing your mind.
Introducing his sound while exhibiting his own style
Design with the ability to make the crowd go wild
Alvin "Al" Downings, 1916–2000
(Al Downings Jazz Theater, Perkins Elem. St. Petersburg, Fla.
Musician educator and teacher at Gibbs Sr. High, Year 39 to 43)

Sweet Hunger

(It Gets Me High!)

I want your love
And I know it's such a fantasy
Just to look at you
Has to be enough for me
And though you may want me too
I know you will never be free
"To marry me. To marry me"
I think about you dear
Almost all of the time
But. I realize that the thought of us
Together is a precious waste of time
"Still it sooths my mind, fate is kind"
I say hello to you
Every time you pass me by
You smile and say hello
A special twinkle in your eye
"It gets me high. It gets me high"
On a promise of love, that doesn't exist
"It gets me high"
So I have to say good-bye
With a phantom kiss
I can't resist
I can't resist my love
It gets me high!

The Circle of Life

It's never too late
To succeed in what you want to do
It's never too late
As long as there's life and breath in you
It's never too late
To do what you have to do
To make all of your dreams a reality
And to make all of them come true
So don't give in
For the world rotates in a circle
And everyone gets a chance
To reach for the stars and their fantasies
They all go hand in hand

Letter to America!

America, let's be fair; even before the 2008
elections the media has been allegedly hyping up
the idea that the USA deficit was suffering and was
already in the process of going broke or bankrupt
and it didn't help that our former president
decided to give away most of the needed money
to banks and other organizations without a plan, scrutiny,
or consequences just before the election results.
He didn't leave enough money for the incoming
President to work with, this action was done so close
To the obvious election of an African American president that
It makes you wonder, we elected a young, electrifying
Senator, who vowed to fix it for us. We pushed him into
promises to act quickly and demanded that whatever he say
He stick too! Our new President had said and I quote
If we stood by him, that we together could do it.
we asked him for change but we gave him no room or time
for anything but rushed decisions and in rushed decisions
There are flaws. In spite of some of the wealthiest allegedly
trying to take, hoard, or not willing to share in spite of wars
storms, hurricanes, tornadoes, earthquakes, fires, or other
developing dangerous elements and of all these other
circumstances He has made pretty good ones, He's saved us
We have elected a good, level-headed president whom
I believe we can trust, he's a brilliant young man who's
Captured the heart and sprit of most of the world
A man who wanted only to help to make life better
For every American citizen while promoting equality and
Justice for all. Does he sleep? Who knows. Never before
Has a President of the United States been scrutinized almost
to the point of torture because he is the president that wants
To help. President Obama was trusting and believing

In transparency in the election of 2008 because of public
Demand candidates were obligated to give some ideas of
of their plans if elected. He had no idea that transparency
would be used against him in such an ugly way. Was he set
up to have all of his ideas sabotaged? Or nipped in the bud?

Or was it used for a bad purpose instead of the good
purpose that he had in mind when he embraced the idea
Of transparency but instead was planned by others
As a design for him to fail? For this transparency is about
his thoughts his plans to rescue us from this downward
spiraling train our country is on
because of the domino effect that the former president
Had started when he almost brought America to a
screeching halt by closing down six oil refineries costing
Jobs and inflating gas prices, which halted transportation of
Food, machinery, and other necessary equipment vital to
Our survival. Medicine went up 100 percent, doctors, hospitals,
Everything. People lost their property their farms, homes,
Insurance. Their livelihood. Republicans were in control
Why didn't they fix it. In Florida they took money from our public
schools' budgets and gave it to private schools, causing
public-school teachers and other school workers to lose
their jobs because of so-call lack of funds tell him what
you think and trust him to listen, He is offering us
a platform of change we might not agree with everything
He proposed, but he is living up to his part of the promise
Even though the media, the GOP, Tea Party, or whomever
Allegedly shoots down all of his ideas and find ways to
turn us against him. We all know we don't wish to go
backwards. We now have someone in the chair who cares
about us as human beings and not as a statistic. He puts
his ideas out there and wants what's best for us He is
trying to work it out. He knows that there are plenty of
Oppositions and that everything that he wants will not

Pass and that is why he has to change some of his ideas
As he goes along. He's not changing his path he is forced
To find new ones. We love his speech and we voted for him in

Our first American Presidential Family
President Barack H. Obama
His Wife
Our first African American First Lady Michelle Obama.

Mr. G. W. Bush and his cabinet, the Republican party are
All alleged accessories. In the fall of the American deficit while
The very rich filled their pockets

Women's Rights!

Listen, folks, this is no joke
Think for a minute!
Stop letting the Republicans
The media and others control our minds
If we spend our money, if we let it flow
Businesses will be able to hire people
The economy will grow
The extra money for Obama health care
That we might have to pay, is not worth
Throwing our liberty away
President Obama was right
But we didn't join his fight
He knows that
His plans are the essential things to do
All he wants to do is improve "our life!"
It is important
That we women obtain our rights
Let's stick together and join his fight
Even though we may not use them
He's giving access with the right to refuse them
He's giving us a choice, our vote is our voice
Whatever he offers women, they should take
Then no longer would others be able to dictate
We'll have what we need no mistake
Our freedom to choose!
Our equality is the real debate!
Remember women's suffrage?

A Woman's Creed

Just give me a chance
To show what I can do no limitations
And I'll prove my worth to you
Because women are not
Just love machines we can create and
Help build your dreams
This is America!
Just give me a chance to walk with you
To work with you
There's so much in life
We can share and do
Don't tie my hands
Don't hold me down and
I'll make you proud to keep me around
Grant us equality with no competitive attitude
Whether we are up to your standards
Or we fall short and be proud of what we do
We are doing it for you too.
Just let us help you, be happy, be fair
Let us stand by your side
And together in unity, we will fight to survive!

Women in America's Outcry!

As a citizen in the United States
We the women in America
Have a lot to say
About our equality
Why do you do us this way
Why do you treat us like
We don't count
Why can't we earn
The same dollar amount
Why do you
Cheat on us in every dime
When we have worked
The same length of time
We have to leave our kids at home; sometimes alone
After working eight hours every day
To take on another job
Why is it this way!
Using our family's quality time
In order to supplement our pay
Risk losing our children
Because we are paid less
And because of these factors
The judge says he's best? "Duh!"

Undercover Abortions

How soon we forget
All the tragedies that occur
With no legal abortion rights
Is it now just one big blur
When women and young girls' bodies
Were found in back alleys
In hotel rooms and suites
Because they were forced
To get an abortion from
Some quack on the street
Who claimed they knew how
But only butchered and maimed
These poor unfortunate women and girls
As well as the babies they claim
Two lives lost instead of one
Bleeding to death
Until the next morning sun
Too scared to go
To the hospital for treatment
Too weak to get help
For they knew they would go to jail
If their secret was not kept
God is forgiving!
{I don't condone unnecessary abortions}

Religious Poetry
IV Poems

Heavenly Bliss!

Together our hearts
Are sewn with love
Shining light
Radiates from above
Together our lives
Will always be
Trusting loving
Eternally!
A glimpse of heaven
Is foreseen
Our beautiful wedding
Every man's dream
And with this step
We honor our King
Our hearts will wear
Our wedding rings!

God's Most Precious Gift to Man

God made the world
As beautiful as can be
Then man in his image
He created Adam
Wise and strong
Saw that he was lonely
Didn't want him to be alone
God made Eve from Adam's rib
The greatest gift he had to give
Created from his body
So that Adam could see
That a part of man
Woman would always be
(This gift to Adam was after his first)
most precious gift
The gift of life and breath!

He Gave His Son!

Our God's so good to you and me
He let his son die to set our souls free
He gave his son's life for our eternity
He let his son Jesus die on the cross
So that our souls would not be lost
He'd made a way for us to be saved
He let his son die and raised him
From the grave
And as he journeyed to glory
He paved our way!

The Mother of Civil Rights

(Ms. Rosa Parks)

First woman of color to lay in state
On Capitol Hill
First woman to ever lay in state
To everyone's will
The mother of Civil Rights
Ms. Rosa Parks
The woman who said no
And set off the spark
That changed the laws of bigotry
And won everyone's heart
We salute you
For living your part
You are a state of art

A House That God Keeps

A more impressive place
I couldn't find
Than the deeper life ministry
As it brings to mind
Experiences I've had
That knocked me off my feet
In the House of David
On one of Tampa's street
Such beautiful and grateful souls
That were rescued through faith
From some of life's greatest holes
Some had dug themselves so deep in sin
That they couldn't get out once they were in
Until they heard through Dr. M. B. Jefferson
God's holy shout
Repent! Repent! God must have said
Follow my criteria for you have been saved
I have blessed you and changed your ways
Welcome to
The deeper life ministries
In my holy praise
For surely God must have chosen
This fine man to serve as messenger
to carry out his holy plan
To bring in sheep who lost their way
Through prostitution, homosexuality,
or crack cocaine
Amid violence sometimes death
of their fellowman

Homeless people who courted defeat
No food no help they lived off the streets
those who had lost their way or strayed
Just got in too deep
He gathered them in God's wayward sheep
To a safe haven in the House of David
That God keeps

On World Peace

Sometimes I sit and I think about
All of the things that causes so much doubt
I wonder about our fellowman and why each country
Can't come up with the same plan of putting love and peace
First in all of our minds while joining together and building
A better place for all mankind
Stop the prejudices and hate against color and race
Try to help each other and love every face
We know that every country has individual needs
Why are some left to suffer and die why are they to bleed
As hands have stretched out together to prevent terrorism
Countries should blend their minds together in heroism
No one should suffer from lack of water
Hear their cry!
No child should suffer from diseases caused by starvation
And be left to die. The way that the world treats the Haitians
Who is to blame? It is a terrible thing that we do
Shame! Shame! Shame!
In Haiti a well as certain parts of Africa, especially in Africa
Water pipes needs to be laid down soil to irrigate
Help them to get food and water help them to compensate
Give these people a chance at life stop the greed and hate
Show them love teach them to use rock sand or wood
To build their homes help them to build their dwellings
So that they may be cool or warm
If all nations pulled together in unity
This would be by far a better world
For you, them, he, she, and me

My Haitian Dilemma!

Haiti!
A country of people that I have
spent a lifetime crying over because
They risk their lives to come to good
Ole America the land of plenty for opportunities
and freedom and are turned back
around into the dangerous turmoils that
they risked going through in order to get
here facing starvation and death on their
makeshift boats
Plus the weather the threat of sharks
Or other sea animals over turning their boats
They are either very brave, desperate
or pushed to the brink of insanity for them
to want to take that journey or perhaps
No one ever came back and that is why
they still think that if they make it here
that they would be safe?

America, Our Training Ground

America is our training ground
For all the world to see
The window to the world
Tranquility for all races
And all creeds
Every land has its people
With their own culture
But it is not to be
For fate is bringing us together
It is our destiny!
For all of the differences in the world
Is to become one in love
Without hate or jealousy
We will live together on this earth
In peaceful harmony

Life in America!

America is the most beautiful country there is to see
With people of all colors and of every nationality
The thoughts and ideas that surrounds it
Makes it almost magical
America is the dream of every human being
we can't resist
The thought of freedom and the liberties that
We possess
And through our voices (our votes) we exist
We can help to create all or most of the good things
That we wish
We can travel on almost any mode of transportation
If we're in the mood
We have foods of desire freedom of worship and
Homes that we choose
We have Internet, iPod, cable TV, entertainment,
Religious freedom, freedom of speech
Access to the news
And music to soothe the soul and the mind
Beginning with spirituals from way back in time
A cry in the air for whatever you want it to be
And though people have their differences
They all share similarities
They all share the essence of
Life in America!

The Affirmative Action Plan

(It's a Welcome!)

Before affirmative action
Was put into plan
Biased people ruled this land
People who didn't love every color and face
Was prejudiced against certain cultures and race
They intentionally worked at keeping
African Americans down used them abused them
Kicked them around kept them from learning
Everything they could know for they were in charge
And didn't want them to mentally grow
A heartless act yes indeed that's why an affirmative
action plan was in need
Some may call it affirmative access
But to the Black race
It's the surest hope for success and
To being treated with dignity
Fairness and their equal rights
That they've earned through
All of our national and international world fights
While trying to secure other countries'
Civil Rights

My Diamond in the Rough!

(Vincent Sims)

He's my diamond in the rough
He's always there
When the going gets tough
He's always there
When I'm in need
Extending a helping hand
Until I succeed
Always a smile across his face
He calms me down when I'm misplaced
Yes he's my diamond
My diamond in the rough
And I'm proud to say
A heart of gold
When he was born
They broke the mold
He strums a guitar
He can make it talk
He can make it sing
He's one of the best on musical strings
I can always count on him
When to me life seems unfair
I can call him on the phone
And in a moment he's there
Always looking after me
A blessing in disguise
A man with a friendship
That carries no ties
Thank you, Vincent
I'll always love you.

Beware of the Friendly Touch

(A True Story)

I once had a friend who was gay
I asked him what made him that way
He replied I can't pretend
I think it was because
I had no female friends
My dad would take me
Everywhere that he went
It was always with men
That's how our time was spent
He said he was about five
When his feelings kicked in
If touched in certain places
He would tingle and grin
It was a scary feeling
And he didn't like it very much
Yet at the age of five
It was from a man's touch
He said he couldn't help it
Men was all that he would see
They were always feeling kissing
Touching on a young boy like he
Who never knew his mother
She left them long ago
He had seen his father crying
In pain
And hoped his mom would
Soon come home again
His dad was not gay
But he had kept the women away
A trying time for a little boy

Who was shy and had little to say
The only people for him to trust
Were men
And all of his companions were
His dad's friends
Growing up he was vulnerable
And impressionable
Got used to his father's friends
Their kisses, their touch
He didn't know how it started
And didn't know when the love began
For some men are just like women
Compassionate and sweet
Easy to fall in love with
Especially by a child in heat
And especially if the men are
And, generous and more
Available to meet

I Went Slimming, I'm Trimming: I'm Swimming, I'm In Style

Putting it away buffet style
Pizza and taco for that extra mile
Too many hamburgers, too much cake
Ate lots of french fries drank milk shake
Got kind of bulgy big mistake
But I did a turnabout I escaped
I went slimming
I'm swimming
I'm trimming
I'm in style
Now I eat a little hamburger
Very little cake
Lots of fruits and veggies
Every day
Drink plenty of water
Take me a swim
Two days a week
Work out at the gym
Walk around the park
Get plenty of rest
Now I'm at the weight
That I like best
Cause I went slimming
I go swimming
I'm trimming I'm in style
Now I get myself a burger
Drink a cup of tea
Check myself in the mirror
Cause it's all about me

Heavenly Bodies!

If there are any heavenly bodies
Walking upon this earth
Raylinda Elaine Morrow (my niece)
With a radiant smile like the sun
Would have to have been one
For she devoted her whole life
To loving and working for Jesus
Spreading the word of God
Teaching people
In order to set their souls free
A person who never stopped
Until her work was done
And then too soon for us
God called her home
Even at her burial ceremony
On a beautiful sunshiny day
Her loving spirit was in the air
We could feel her presence there
And as we said our last prayer
Suddenly from out of the blue
From the head of her casket
A loud flapping noise
A gust of wind came through
We could hear her wings flapping
Pausing at the end of her casket
While flipping the ground carpet
As she took off to the sky
Headed for the heavens
Her glorious home on high!

She Walked in Grace

(Clara Young, My Friend)

Her time has come
And my friend is gone
She had suffered
But it made her stronger
When I was hurting or in despair
She would call me on the phone
And if I didn't answer
She would come to my home
Like a guarding angel
She was always there for me
She would appear like from nowhere
When I was in distress or need
Helping me comforting me
Doing her good deeds
Clara, your spirit is in thin air
So many miss you but it's fair
God wants you
He's called you there
Clara carried a song in her heart
Always a smile on her face
She gave her soul to Jesus
And walked in his grace
Clara, I know you're in Heaven
You gave up sin
Long before the end

It Was a Good Thing

(Bringing Together the Mizell Tribe)

It was a good thing
When Will Mizell was alive
And we celebrated the family tribe
Along with his brothers and sisters
Who stood right by his side
It was a good thing
It was a good thing
Until one Christmas Day
God called Will Mizell's number
And took my grandfather away
On Christmas Day in 1975
God called Edith (Mizell) Daniels of
Will and Annie (Parish) Mizell's tribe
My mother, their oldest child
The angels came to get her and
They met her with a smile
It was a good thing
Started by Aunt Dorothy
The search of the Mizell family tree
What a wonderful thing she did
To unite our family
And when she elected to step aside
And chose cousin Eunice
To host the Mizell tribe

Sierra D.

(Performs with the Sounds of Soul, Act 111
and Female leader of the Bus Stop Band)

Sixteen-year-old Sierra D.
A performer with an act
So spiritually uplifting
An outstanding stage presence
So unique that
Every time you watch her
It's a special treat
She's a phenomenal talent
From the city of St. Pete
Born a Floridian flower
A fragrance you can't resist
She's a performer
It pays not to miss
She's dynamic, electrifying
Exciting yet sweet
Still her love her innocence
Her passion for music
Will bring you to your feet

A Proclamation of a Prostitute

I once met a woman
Who was a prostitute on the street
She had one child and must provide
A place for them to sleep
She says she couldn't hold a job
Still they have to eat
She loves her child
And it's a little boy
She says he's her life
He's her pride her joy
She acknowledges that
It is hard out there
And she has to take a lot
Stressing that it's no pleasure
Having to work the blocks
She has to avoid the police
And other vices on the beat
Diseases, bad clients, sometimes
Other prostitutes that she meet
It causes her to drink sometimes
To do the things that she's done
For in reality all she wants
Is a good husband and
A father for her son

A Home for a Friend

I've seen her
Pushing a grocery cart
Up and down the street
Filled with all kinds of stuff
Cans, rags, and maybe
Something for her to eat
Such a sad look upon her face
It seemed to warrant an embrace
And for the girl she was
There is not a trace
I saw her asleep
In her basket one day
I asked her to come with me
I know a place for you to stay
So paranoid she jumped
On to her feet
Brushed down her clothes
And started to retreat
She was a neighbor of mine
Was once very kind
But the use of crack
Had taken over her mind
No longer responsible
For the things that she does
So I'll take her to a place
Filled with compassion and love
The House of David
On one of Tampa's street

A Recovering Alcoholic

He yelled and screamed
All of the time
Always drinking and smoking
His love for the booze was blind
He had frightened his wife
And children away
And regrets his actions
Up to this day
For now he is sober
And can clearly think
Realizes his troubles started
From his very first drink
It's too late for him now
His family is gone
Never to return again
He's now on his own
He says that
Time heals all wounds
But you don't forget
And losing his family
He will always regret

The Life You Save May Be Your Own!

To many people
Don't stop to think
How many lives
Are in the hands of that drink
It may be your child
Your wife
Your husband or you
Who loses their life
Because of a drink or two
People under the influence
Shouldn't be on the street
Driving a vehicle
Because their mind is weak
So don't drink and drive
Push that drink aside
Help us to keep our families alive
And let common sense be your only guide

Little Girl!

(Abstinence Is Your Best Friend)

Little girl, wait to get your baby
Don't become a mama too soon
Keep your panties up
And your dress tail down
Tell the beggar you have no room
Tell him that your mind
Is filled with thoughts of
Education and financial security
And you want to finish school
Tell him that you want to earn your degrees
And sex without marriage is against the rules
Tell him he should keep his zipper up
And his pants around his waist
Go to school, pursue a career
And learn a trade that really pays
Tell him that you choose to practice abstinence
For it is the best way that you know
Not to get a disease
Not to have a baby out of wedlock
Not to make yourself out to be a whore

Think!

A girl having a baby
Trying to please some boy
Messing up her life
Thinking she'll be his wife
When to him she's just another toy
Little girl, think what you'll be missing
If you have a baby too soon
Think of all the milk and Pampers
You'll have to buy
Think of all the strange times
That your baby will cry
You won't have time
To talk on the phone
Most of your friends
Will leave you alone
You'll miss your graduation
Your senior prom
And most of the time
You'll be home all alone

Choose Life!

If you don't truly have an understanding
Of what life is about
You will more than likely choose abortion
Thinking that it is your only way out
You will make a decision based on unfortunate
Circumstances and your mind will shut down
Because you will feel alone in your troubles
While assuming there's no help to be found
So you make a decision based on fear and loneliness
That helps to bring miseries
And a life that's filled with stress

A Predator's Playground!

Protect your child
From the Internet
It's a predator's playground
Pedophiles are on the loose
Waiting to track your child down
Don't make it easy for them to score
No Internet in the bedroom
Or behind other closed doors
But a place where everyone can be
Monitor their activities
Don't let your child
Be sucked into
The predator's raging sea
For family unity
Is the best protection
To keep them molested free

Protect Your Children!

Don't let people buy your children
You give them what they need
Give them your love your time
Security and affection
Don't leave them to be
Tempted by greed
Never let anyone
Give money or gifts
Directly to your child
For everything must
Be done through you
Say this is your way of
Protecting your children
And is something that
All parents should do

Resentment Can Lead You to Disaster

I've always resented authority
I got angry when my parents said no to me
Don't do this, don't do that
And so I made a pact with myself
That I'd do the best to that I can to be free
To run away to leave them behind
And be what I wanted to be
Before I even finished high school
I was standing there saying I do to you
When my parents told me no
I felt I just had to go
So I would always sneak outside the door
Now what a lesson I have learned
When you have a hard head, you'll get burned
I thought marriage was for me
Never had such misery
This was not an escape to be free
I'm going back home, I'm going home and gladly
Let my parents chastise me

The Green-Eyed Monster

Don't let the green-eyed monster get you
Don't let it turn you on
Don't let things it says upset you
Follow your heart, it's your song
It's just a green-eyed presence
Trying to make you blue
With those devil eyes that it has
Trying to put a spell on you
Don't give it a chance to get into your mind
Watch out for its tempting smile
Its' goal is to gain a little inch at a time
Then take you for a country mile
Don't let the green-eyed monster get you
Don't let it rule your mind
Don't give it a chance to screw you up
And everything will work out fine
Jealousy is its specialty
It will set you off if it can
Dis it off if you see it coming
Don't give it a helping hand
Get rid of
That green-eyed monster!
If jealousy
Is not in your plan
Get rid of
The green-eyed monster!
And your realm of Peace will expand!

Slogans on Drug Abuse

Saturday morning, 3:00 a.m.
February 26, 1999
by Jacquelin D.
A.k.a Bennie Adams

I.   The only dope worthwhile is the dope on education

11.   Heroin, smack. Crank or crack or crack cocaine will drive you crazy: drive you insane

111.   Dope is a joke. Live in the real world

IV.   Crack is a violation of your body, the end of your life

V.   Beware of the dealers

VI.   Crack spells bankruptcy

V11.   Do you work to give your money to drug dealers? Watch out, they are lurking for you

V111.   The zombie says, a zombie you will be, a Zombie you will be if you use substances of drug abuse. You'll wind up just like me

IX.   Ditch drugs, don't wait. The way out is to rehabilitate

X.	The skeleton said, "If want your body to look like mine, then by all means you are on the right track using crack.

XI.	Drug abuse is the Yellow Brick Road to poverty

XII.	What is the surest road to poverty? Answer: drug abuse

XIII.	Crime is the first-class passage to jail

XIV.	A felony is the first step to destruction

Be Hard Core

(Say no to Drugs)

Kids, listen up!
To what I have to say
No, don't give in
Don't throw your life away
You have a good mind, use it
Don't do nothing to abuse it
Say no to him
If the drug man comes your way
Drugs are a mean ol' war machine
They will cut you down
Take away your dreams
They will have you crying
Ducking and hiding
Running till the break of day
Sleeping on the ground
In bushes all around
And for a few minutes
Of pleasure you'll pay
Drugs will make
A rich man pay
Drugs will have him
Sleeping out of doors
They have no pity on anyone
Drugs will make you forget
How to have fun
Say no if the drug man
Comes your way
Say no you refuse
To live that way!

Stay Away From the Devil's Clutches

Don't, don't, don't touch drugs
It will hurt you so
It will get you in the devil's clutches
And won't let go
You won't know your tomorrows
It will fill you full of sorrow
And the ones you love
Will suffer even more
Turn your back on the evil hand
Get away from those drugs
And run as fast as you can
Just close your mind to it
Everyone and his sister can do it
Resist those drugs
Stay a sensible man
When you see them
Standing on the street
Trying to sell crack
To everyone they meet
Remember, no money will you keep
They will take everything that you own
From your head to your feet
So fight, fight, fight the best way you can
Say no, no, no until they understand
Education you will find
Will build you a better mind and you won't
Have to worry about crawling a crooked line

Fighting Crime

(Get Involved)

Get involved, help your sisters and your brothers
Hear their cry when they're screaming in pain
Show the love that you have for one another
Give them help, don't just stand there in vain
If you know that they're being assaulted
Or that they are victims of crime
Don't try to be indifferent
Don't try to hold out
Let's break this code of silence
Tell what it's all about
Call the law let them do what they are paid for
And clean the streets of the violence we share
But they are not to hurt innocent people and
Police brutality is not why we put them there
Instead let's interact with the officers to show
Our interest
Let's show our integrity and how much we care
Let's join together to fight crime
And perhaps in our working together
We will all find some peace of mind

Fighting Crime

(Get Some Help for Me)

I am your sister
I am your brother
This is America!
I am your family
If you hear my cry
Please reach out to me
Don't let this person injure my body
Or take away a piece of me
Don't let them put me in the ground
Or cause me misery
Don't let them hurt me
Or I might be your worse nightmare
Not fit for anyone to see
So act with love concern and care
Show some sympathy
Call the police call the cops
Get some help for me!

Fighting Crime

(Call the Police)

If you hear me holler
If you hear me scream
Call the police
Call the police
This is not a dream
If I scream and holler
When you hear my pain
Call the police
Call the police
This is not a game
Violence is a danger
Violence is a crime
Call the police
Call the Police
Don't waste precious time

Description of a User

(A Victim of Crack Cocaine)

You walk real fast
Like you got no bones
Like Jell-O in a Jell-O dish
Your back is swayed
And you walk on your toes
You remind me of a jellyfish
Bloodshot eyes and your pupils are big
You grunt just like a grown-up pig
Sometimes I hear you crying in agony
Are you sorry for what you did
So paranoid that you walk back and forth
Thinking that the cops
Are hanging around your door
You think there are people
Hiding under your sheets
You even think they're hiding
In the shoes off your feet
You pick little pieces up off the floor
You're running out of crack
And you're searching for more
Man oh man!
What have you done?
You've ruined your life
Now the pressure's on
Don't give up hope, give up the dope
You have to do this yourself on your own
When the dope man comes send him home

Buyer Beware!

Growling like a wolf man
Looking like you're insane
That is what drugs do to you
You'll become
That you never ever knew
Drugs will have you doing things
You thought you'd never do
Sleeping in the outdoors
Making out with other whores
Better be careful because if you're not
Aids is out there causing rot
Run all the time can't get no sleep
Barely able to stop and eat
Please help me!
Oh Mother, Mother!
Don't let the drug man get my brother!
Sister, sister run away!
This is no place for you to stay
Get away from the drugs I say
Your body and mind will waste away
Your whole world will go astray
And you will lose all you working money!

Evil Is the Woman's Greed

Her husband would repeatedly tell her, "No, hon,
I don't want you to do this. It is wrong." And as if
possessed by some evil force, she would angrily
shout at him, "For goodness's sake, man, why don't
You shut the **** up, you've turned into a worthless
nothing, you're spineless. Where is your backbone?"
Instead of standing up to what he believed
He submitted to her will instead of God's will and
his home was taken over by the evil spirit that had
consumed his wife. He felt he had broken his
His covenant over his family, become a broken man.
He became afraid to open the door. His body
shaking at every knock. Every phone call caused him
to jump. He couldn't sleep. Still, with every passing day
he would cringe knowing that his wife in spirit was
no longer with him. For the demons had
taken over and greed was her leader.
The smell and thought of money was her guide
Her husband was a Christian man with a conscious
Who always believed in trying to live right and by the
Word. Despite His Christian upbringing, high morality,
principles, and values. He became so afraid for his
wife and what she was doing that he had allowed
the devil come into their lives and take over.
His compassion for his wife blinded him to the
Word of God. And in his weakness he forgot the power of
prayer and because of his submission to her literally
he was broken down into a mere mass of meat
while she constantly nagged him until finally a heart
attack overcame him. As in his last breath he cried
God forgive me!

Escape Through Poverty

I knew a lady who once had a home
She worked so hard for what she owned
Her husband had left them all alone
She raised their two children after he had gone
Yet her children grew up knowing they belonged
Her daughter grew up to be every man's dream
Her son was captain of the football team
But then one day someone came into her life
It was a man who wanted the lady for his wife
The son was outraged because he was the man
Didn't want no intruders for this was his land
He became so belligerent, he cursed his mom out
And almost every word to her was in a shout
His mom was at the stage wherein she had had enough
Her became bossy and acted very tough
She was at the age where in she could retire
The thought of her fiancée with her just lit up his fire
He flatten her tires because he knew it would hurt
Made it impossible for her to drive to work
Kicked the door down threw fiancée out
And called him a jerk there was no living with him
For her son who now only wanted her money
Was a louse so she decided to move away and
Sell the house
To get away from her son and be left alone
She put herself into a senior citizen's home

Buggin' Susan

One summer afternoon Sue was in the kitchen cooking
When John her husband walked in, saying,
"What's for supper, sweetie?" Susan replied, "Ooh tonight
We're having, spaghetti." John said, "I'll go up and shower."
Susan shouted after him, "Sure, baby,
Dinner will be served soon!" Singing
Sue went into the preparing of his favorite dishes.
Humming la da da da da da da
Then suddenly she spotted a large bug.
It was a roach oh dear! She shouted.
"I'll get you! Ohh! I hate roaches." So
She picked up a fly swatter and hit
The bug, cutting it in half. The two halves
Spun in a circular motion and blended
Making a bigger roach. Sue said,
"Oh my goodness!" And hit the bug again
And again the bug split, made a circle,
Rejoined, and became an even bigger bug
At this point Sue begun to scream
"John, help! Aiiiiiiiiie! Help!"
And all the time she was either
Hitting or hitting at the bug and every
Time she hit it, it would fuse and grow
Larger meanwhile John who was in
The bathroom in the shower heard her
When he stuck his head out of the shower
To get the shampoo grabbed his towel and
Ran toward her voice where he too saw
This monstrous roach on the floor and his wife Susan
all excitedly hitting the bug and screaming in fear

Help! John shoved Susan out of the way
He grabbed the big boiling pot of hot water off the stove
Threw it on the giant roach; the roach started swirling around
In circles faster, faster than ever before so fast it was like the
Eye of a twister. Then there was a silence, the roach lay dead
On its back, feet in the air, it was just another dead bug!

Two Sisters

I loved Gracie Mae Mobley
And her sister BB Bennett
They were very important in
My life.
They gave me a sense of
Belonging and eased
A lot of my strife.
No matter what I wanted
Or what I did they never
Seemed to mind. Gave me
A choice of what I wanted
Always treated me kind.
Gracie Mae and BB.
My cousins, my aunts,
My second moms,
My friends. Told me
That my mom
Edith was their cousin
Their sister always until
The end. And then
They gave me a smile
Said I was welcome
Anywhere they were
Because I was Edith's
Child.
Gracie Mae and BB
Was as sporty as they
Could be.
Dressed to kill
Extra high heels

Furs and diamond rings
Exciting enough in any
Case to make any man's
Heart sing.
They loved the way
That I walked said
I had a special little strut
They often would have
Me model for them
It would always cheer them up
They said that my
Walk was for real
It happens naturally
And that if they could
Choose the way that
They walk
They would do it
Just like me.
They loved cousins
Ruth Williams and
Marie Adams
They hung out together
They were buddies
You see
They lived a good life
And had good times
Of happy memories
Sometimes they
Would stay up and
Talk right through
The night
Reminiscing

About old times
Until the morning
Light.
I would lay my head
On one of their laps
And they would
Continue talking
Right through my naps
Oh how they loved to
Talk they had so much to
Say about exciting
Experiences that they
Shared back in time
Back during their day
Reminiscing of good times
Gone by
Dreaming of
Another day
The things those two sisters
Had in common
They are not enough words
To say

The Bush Era!

They turned the world around
Left little money to be found
Really turned our deficit around
Now our country is spiraling down
They got the greedy itch
Threw America in the ditch
Closed down six oil refineries
Sent our jobs overseas
Poverty climbed up
One hundred degrees
Doubled the cost of medicine
And our families lost a lot of kin
Gave public schools a budget cut
Many lost their jobs made life tough
After cutting the school budget
Maybe in half
Fired many workers
And teaching staff
Took budget money from
The poor gave to the rich
(Private schools)
And now our Public schools are in a fix
Stopped transportation in its tracks
Lost lots of businesses
Didn't bring them back
Property, farms, homes
Everything was gone
All because of those inflating bank loans
The GOP's ballooning effect
Instead of having our backs
Stabbed us in the feet
Causing thousands of people

To beg for food, sleep in the street
For President Obama
It really sucks
To have to clean this mess
Allegedly was made up
No president ever had
To handle so much
A landslide of problems
Caused by man
A domino effect
That's ruined this land
A party in American government
Who allegedly
Sacrificed their people
And now
Won't lend a hand
Who's trying to prove
They are superior
We understand, only
We don't want to live this way
We want equality, liberty
And justice every day
We want our right to choose
Especially Women's Rights!
We may not ever use them
But we don't want to lose them
Women! Don't be misled by issues!
Vote for President Obama!
A vote for us to choose!

About Abortion-Rights Elimination

(A Different Perspective)

If we abolish women's abortion rights
More shysters, charlatans, and butchers
Will come into light
Capitalizing on a situation
That most women would be forced to take
The killing of more mothers and babies
By people who are phony
By people who are fake
Promising something they can't deliver
Just the thought of all those people dying
Just gives me the shivers
It will be because of the law of the land
The system will be responsible
For lives that are lost
Forsaking women's abortion rights
At any cost
It will be on our hearts and our hands
Some quacks making a fortune
For things they cannot do
The system would have failed these females
Who else could they turn to?
Abortion without sterilization, no supervision?
Can we live with this?
Our laws, our system reopening doors for
these things to exist?

The Ronnetts

(My Cousins, the Divas)

Remember the Ronnetts
Three enchanting beauties
That swept throughout the nation
Like a storm
Embracing everyone
With outstretched arms
Singing "Be my Baby"
"Be my Baby"
With poofed-up hairdos
Long black lashes
They generated a style
Where in women and teenagers
All went wild
Eyelashes dripping
Mascara everywhere
The world was having fun
New looks new hair
To Ronnie and Nedra
We thank you, we love you
We still care
(In memory of Estell Bennet 1942–2009)

Cindy Mizell!

Diva Cindy Mizell, my first cousin
Was background singer for Luther Vandross
And Freddie Jackson for years
Gliding through their repertoires of happy
And soulful tears
With her voice blazing her glory behind their music
They couldn't go wrong
For Cindy graduated to a hit album of her very own!
(*I've Had Enough*)

Ronald "Winky" Wright!

Young, handsome, and growing strong
Our shining star, Ronald "Winky" Wright
He fought his way to new heights
St. Petersburg's own
World boxing champion
Is making Florida proud
Has put us on the international map
Let's hear it out loud
We love You, Winky!
(Won the IBF junior middleweight title at the Fantasy Springs in Indio, California)

Rosa Parks

A woman with tired feet
Who sat down to rest
Caused a change in the world
Contributing
To the Civil Rights success
She was told to give up her seat
To someone who was white
Even though it was the law
It definitely wasn't right
She had paid her money
For a seat inside a bus
That she rode
And was ordered to move
To the rear
So tired and weary from
A hard day's work
Refused, to give up
Her space and wallow
In hurt and fear
And from her fight
Came a movement
In Civil Rights
That made
That law disappear

Ride on a Rainbow

(My Oprah Song)

She's a ride on a rainbow
To your wildest dreams
She's the queen of the talk show Hosts
The greatest on the scene
With outstretched arms she'll embrace you
With all her worldly charm
And take you on an angel walk
through a world where you belong
The world of Oprah, Oprah
She loves you so much
Oprah, Oprah
The one with the Midas touch
She gave away cars
Made famous stars
Beat the cattlemen in their own beef
But most of all
She made the call
That President Obama would be chief
Oprah, Oprah she's a special girl
Oprah, Oprah, we've enjoyed your world

Katrina's Aftermath!

During Katrina's thunderous approach
There were strong winds, swelling waters
And to much water pressure wearing
The levies out, causing the levies to break
People waiting and wondering
How much more could the levies take
Before they all break into, how much longer
Must they wait to get help water and food
How long before they are rescued
Believing that it wouldn't be long
For this is America their home
And they knew that
These United States take care of its own
And that we are the greatest country in the world
We take care of our citizens
And their lives were at stake
But how much longer would it take
After seven days of the terrible stench in the air
Dead bodies floating in the water
Because no one seemed to care
Such a horrific sight, it was a graveyard there
A beautiful city wiped out by a flood because
They had no help to get out, no buses, no helicopter
No National Guard, no Coast Guard, no call to arms
What was this all about? Strong winds, swelling waters
A whole city about to drown, poor people screaming
For help and dying with no help to be found
Six days one after the other as the levies broke
And New Orleans choked
Plenty of time for rescue
But no one seemed to have a clue
Six days had come and gone

Were they all alone?
Did they all have to die that way?
In the dawning of another day a miracle appeared
Help had arrived!
Ten thousand people had not died
As the world had feared
Because God is the Master Creator
And it is in his hand whether man live or die
In his master plan

Eyewitness!

Once Oprah had a show
On what people remember
How much they know
How much they observe
And how much they let go
Eyewitnesses she wanted to claim
For an experiment a test it was just a game
To see what people can see
And how good is their memory
If they witness a crime or robbery
In a crowd of people this was done
They staged this game for everyone
And though they were actors and many could see
Only one person had clear memory
It proved that some people see what they want to see
Others imagine what they think it should be
And though one eyewitness statement was true
Other eyewitnesses didn't have a clue

Angela Bassette

Oscar nominee! Best actress!
Another internationally famous person
Helping to bring St. Petersburg, Florida,
To the world's attention
So that we don't have to settle for
An honorable mention an example that
Our city has talent galore
A perfect example of achievements in store
One of the goals you can obtain in life
If you work hard and become successful
Enough to knock down that door
The multitalented Angela Bassette
A ravishing Floridian flower
Followed her dreams and became the lady of the hour
Proving to everyone that Florida is unique
She is one of the special ones that adorns its chemistry
A Floridian flower from St. Pete
Miss Angela Basset
Our precious academy awards nominee
In "What's Love Got to Do with It"
Was Tina Turner gave the performance of her life
A sure winner for the Oscar but?

Pro-Choice and Alternatives

Don't take away a woman's right to choose
Give her alternatives that she can't refuse
Why do women wish to abort? Because of rape
Bad health, fear of possible death
Because they're all alone, left on their own
With no one to care, nothing seems fair
Caught up in a time of grief and despair
No money on hand, the loss of a man
Why not offer a program
That comes straight from the heart
Teaching that abortions are not very smart
A one-time special grant, a plan, a guide
Make them know this program is not just a lonely ride
Feed them, shelter them, make them feel at home
Be their family when they think they are all alone
Fill them with pride through this risk that they take
Offer all methods of birth control
Free tubules and for men vasectomies
Give them every aspect in life to remain abortion free
Guys should be liable for the babies that they make
And taken through parenting classes too.
To learn what's really at stake
And what they are required to do
They should be taught the sanctity of marriage
And what children require, no more reproduction
From sexual lust and desire
Men should be held responsible
For the part that they play
With requirements to visit

At least two hours in a day
Should be made to contribute
Toward their child's success
To make each day of their life
A day of happiness

Choosing a Winner

If I had my choice of whom I'd rather be
It would be Oprah because she inspires me
She's a women with a charismatic style
With great determination and a winning smile
She's intelligent intellectual so real and warm
And like so few filled with loving charm
She has a heart of gold and talent to behold
And she's given me the courage to try to be bold
I've watched her struggles
To win the fight of weight control and
She's out of sight' she'll get it right
I've said so many times that
I hope she stay
Giving us advice the Oprah way
The woman is together
Class act of today!

The Flight of the Butterfly Ballot (2000-2007)

Allegedly!
Because of the fluke intentionally or not
That announced Bush winner
Before the voting had stopped
And then be told by the media hey! It's on again
Then announce to the public Al Gore wins
And then turned around and announced
It's George Bush again now what a great gimmick
If this thing was planned if you were a president elective
With the ball in your hand
And for ballots to disappear or be misplaced
Whatever is happening to the presidential race
Lots of funny things seemed to be going on
Causing the voting results to turn out wrong
At a crucial time in Florida when
The Democrats came on strong and the names on
The butterfly ballot were not where they belong
A small discrepancy one might have thought
About this voting machine that was newly bought
Not lining the candidates name and punch lines
Equal as they should be making it difficult for
People who have trouble trying to see
And even for some people who voted religiously
A trick on the butterfly ballot that could confuse your mind
If you were not aware and couldn't see it in time
Would cause you to make a mistake and you would punch
A second time and even though you would have to punch again
People could see your intent because all ballots with two punches
Would have been Gore for president for he was the only leading
Candidate whose name was out of place and no one would cast
Two votes for the other candidates who were not seriously in
the race

In Florida, when they first prematurely announced that Bush wins,

The polls shut down they wouldn't let the voters in. They turned them out

Wouldn't let them stay and that's how so many votes got whisked away

And then the media announced Al Gore had won that was a dirty trick

Someone was just having fun, soon after another announcement was in

The making and the media said that Bush had won I thought,

Why were they faking? Strange things started happening they began

Stopping cars in the street only Black men did they seek

Trying to prevent a Republican defeat. It was like a robbery

So many ballots found along the wayside not being counted

As they should be. So many Democrat votes thrown away

What a mockery. Vice President Gore would never have

Stooped to that kind of trickery to win the presidential race

But if he saw a better way over that is the one he would embrace

As he did when he found out that his party's ballots

Were being taken away and he vowed he would stand firm

For our rights to our vote and for all Americans to have their say

He had won the election by popular vote that crucial day but

The electoral college took it away

Flight of the butterfly ballot!

The Election-Day Blues

Since November 7th
I've been sad inside
Because Mr. Gore
The president of my choice
Was taken for a ride
But to Mr. G. W. Bush
I apologize
For this river of tears
That flows from my eyes
This heartbreaking news
That I carry inside
And although I know
That you're probably innocent
I still cried
Because to strip us of our vote
Our voice
Is to strip me of my pride
And so alone in solitude
In private in Florida
I cried and cried and cried

A Shout-Out For Whoopi!

Whoopi Goldberg
A woman with true grit, wit, and
A determination that won't quit
When Whoopi Goldberg debuted
We all knew another superstar was born
So talented, so down to earth
A beauty with an arrogance all her own
She stood out, she had her own style
She was so unique
She had everything except an Oscar
To make her life complete
But like all Black actresses before her
She was nominated but never chosen
The Academy Awards decor?
Or was it their motto against Black actresses
Only one had won before
Being a superior actor as she were
And a great performer with attitude
She kicked down that door
She gave the kind of performances
That no one could ignore
Ms. Goldberg made a difference in this kind of art
They couldn't deny her the Oscar for she was too smart
But she broke that barrier, she got her star!

Dr. Maya Angelou

One of the greatest poets ever to compete
Very well spoken, has earned a doctorate degree
And her poetry will bring you up on your feet
A legend, an icon in poetic literature
She is poetry in motion, you can be sure

A Rejuvenation of Life!

Thanks for the face-lift
That keeps you looking young
Thanks for the surgeons
Who have the ability to perform
And thanks to your family
And friends
Who help to build your self-esteem
And thanks to that special someone
In your life
Who helped to carry out your dreams

We Must Learn to Understand

There was a child born
With two sex organs
As everyone could see
His parents were so shocked
All they could mutter was
How could this be? How could this be?
They thought about how much
Their child would suffer if left in this situation
They wanted to save their child from
Physical embarrassment and mental frustration
And so they relented to society's demands
Regretfully allowing a premature castration
They never had the time to fully understand
What kind of situation they had on hand
A child growing up and they had yet to see
Would it be male or female like me
Uh-oh, what did they do?
Did they choose the right organ before
The personality came through?
A male trapped in a female's body
A female trapped in a man's
Things like this can happen
We must learn to understand

Is This the Exchange?

(Question about the Bush Policy before 9/11/2001)

Shutting down oil refineries
Causing gas prices to exceedingly rise
Halting our mode of transportation
Making our nation cry
The price of oil is not up
And yet the cost of gas is sky-high
Eliminating thirty-three oil refineries
Loss of jobs
What does these actions seem to imply?
When he promised the tax cuts
Did that make the price of gasoline soar?
Less gas for more money
Boy, that's hitting our pockets deep
Because if the gas prices inflates any higher
We will have no place to sleep

Natural Rights

I believe in women's rights
And that we should be protected
From people we are forced to fight
To make laws to help and protect us
Would certainly heighten our plight
For more opportunities and Freedom
To win our
Natural rights!
Ladies, it is better to have them
And not need them
Than to need them
And not have them
Opportunity knocks but once
Think about it!

Helping Because He Can

Pastor Jessie Jackson
He stood out as a young activists
First black man to run for president
A man of civil action who walked with
Dr. M. L. King Jr. and others upon this land
While crusading to put Civil Rights and
Affirmative action into plan
Born a public-relations man was trusted
And was often sought by many nations
To help to settle some situations
Because he is wise and takes a peaceful stand
He fights for the rights of people in need
And won't give up until he succeed
A man blessed with love and valor
Always striving to help the other fellow
Helping because he can
Jessie Jackson a man of great influence
Born a public-relations man
Who was sought out by rulers of
Other continents to help to settle
Any situation that they didn't seem to understand
Who fights for the Civil Rights of people in need
And won't give up until he succeeds
Blessed with love and valor
Always striving to help the other fellow

Executive Lady, Executive Oprah

The woman of today
Executive Oprah, we salute you
The women of today
Your name will go in history
Among women whose paved the way
As every woman you fight
The battle of the bulge
And that's our greatest fight
It's a feat that goes on and on
From morning into the night
You're an artist in your field
An icon, an actress, a producer
You're our queen
An example that there is success
For every woman's dream
You've beat
The cattlemen's beef allegedly
In their own crooked schemes
You're the executive lady
The talk-show host queen!
You've paved the way
Through tomorrow for
The women of today
You've shown yourself to be
A good person a blessing
In every way you've proven to us
That beauty is not in the size
It comes from the soul
With heart, with a smile
It comes with compassion

Envisioned in your eyes
Real beauty is something
Money cannot buy. Oprah, you're
The queen and we all know why

John F. Kennedy

Father of Integration!
On November twenty-second
Nineteen sixty-three
I was carrying a baby inside of me
President Kennedy was shot and killed
And it seemed for a moment
The whole world stood still
He was shot by a coward
With a bullet from a far
Our chief, our president
Our hero, our star
He was our hope, our choice
And plenty tough
He told Castro enough is enough
If you don't straighten up
You'll have to deal with us
He faced Khrushchev
And backed him down
Because Khrushchev was wrong
And out of bounds
Coming to Cuba
To set up a missile base
Kennedy said no and they both agreed
After talking it over how
They both could succeed
They were wise men
They didn't want to become enemies
They didn't want to fight they wanted to be friends
And in brotherhood unite
Because these two great powers were needed
To keep world peace and to act as world guardian
Until the violence cease

John F. Kennedy was a man of the time
Whom we appreciate, the first president
In my day
Helping to design up a plan to desegregate

Prince of America!

(John Kennedy Jr. as a boy)

John Boy Kennedy
Prince of America
The land where he was born
Eyes wept for him and his family
Through the night until the morn
A salute to you, John Boy
As you saluted your dad
You showed your love,
Respect, and strength
You were a courageous lad
The son of a great president!

Life Savers!

Our soldiers, firemen, medics, and
Coast and National Guards rank number one
Our heroes and heroes, our protectors
Our daughters our sons
Fighting for our country
From dusk to dawn
No prejudices, no hatred
Love on the run
Dedicating their lives
To get the job done

The American Way!

Compassion under fire
An Iraq man carrying a child
Shouting, "My child is injured!"
An American soldier
Also in danger
Grabbing the child
While running to help
Thinking of the child
And not only of himself
Shows compassion
And the humility
Of innocent minds
Although under pressure to fight
Still remains carrying and kind
A perfect example
Of our soldiers today
Like President Obama
To help and to heal
The American Way!

A Man with a Soul

Lyndon B. Johnson
For world freedom
Many Presidents made a start
But it was President Johnson
That stole my heart
He was raised in poverty
And he knew how it was not to be free
President Johnson made a great effort
With the plan drawn up called
The Great Society
It provided African Americans
Their rights and equality fought for by
Great men. He, President Kennedy,
The Father of World Freedom
Dr. Martin Luther King Jr. and
All of the courageous people
Who walked with him side by side
Taking ruthless punishment
Some beaten unmercifully, put in jail
Some even died yet still
They prayed they sang
They took it all in stride
They knew that freedom was inevitable
An essence of human pride
The president was very hurt
Being talked into a war that didn't work
Our world leaders advised him
That South Vietnam was bad
And our world went to war against them
But he found out that we had been had
This realization made him very sad
The Vietnam War had interfered with

His Great Society Plan
When he had been badly advised about
Freedom in another land
For African Americans he gave them their rights
For everything at hand
The rights to all equalities and made a change in this land
To South Vietnam in which he wished to restore
He did what he thought was right he opened our doors
And to his reelection probabilities
He said no more, no more! No more!

Go, Johnny, Go!

Johnny Robinson of St. Pete
Music is his life
Rosetta is his wife
Robinson and Son Studio
A legend in Tampa Bay
Everyone would be musicians
If he had his way
A local producer of talent
That everyone should know
Who's spent most of his life
Introducing and promoting
Talented kids in his musical show
Providing the evidence
By gaining them exposure
And building their confidence
While keeping Tampa Bay entertained
And helping our children to mentally grow
By teaching them to play drums, brass,
Keyboard, and musical strings
High notes, low notes and taught them to sing
For in this musical world that he loves so
In Tampa Bay we chant, "Go, Johnny, go!"
Johnny is better known for his groups
M3 and Act3
Which featured many local stars
For little or no fee

My Fantasy

I went into a club
It was about a quarter to ten
Everybody started starring
From the moment that I walked in
There was this guy on stage
Looking so sweet to me
He was doing his thing
Singing so enthusiastically
He came over to my table
Then he fell onto his knee
Doing a Keith Sweat song
Saying baby baby
Please please please
Whatever the song
I was caught up in his trance
And I felt him hold my hand
As he went into this sexy dance
He said his name was sexy
And his gaze put me into a fix
I felt like - I was being romanced
Even though I knew
It was an entertainers trick
When he moved on
I came back to earth where I belong
There was a note in my hand with
A number for me to phone
I were glad that I went there
For the first time on my own
I was lucky
Because I were able to
Take home my fantasy
Even though I knew
Tomorrow! - Back to reality!

My Image of Princess Diana (As I See Her)

I had to be free, I had to be me
Or whatever it takes for my liberty
I loved my husband, Prince Charles
And that he could see
Though another had his heart
Instead of me
I bore his sons out of love for him
And that was good, the throne is for them
But to be snuffed away, no choice of my own
My duties were automatic, the system was powerful
I couldn't just exist, I had to find my place
I gave it up—on my own—and to some it was wrong
But I had to be strong for I were alone
I had to do what I did, I just couldn't go on
For the love of my people I had to make a start
To show them my love that came from my heart
I wanted to help couldn't think of myself
No longer a princess sitting on a shelf
I may have lost my throne but I've built a home
With my people, their dreams, and dreams of my own

Diana!

Diana, princess of us all
Gave up her throne
For a mighty cause
Of helping people
She saw was in need
She was a great lady
A princess indeed
The Princess of Wales
Who had a heart of gold
A story to be told
And the need to exhale

Pastor Sykes

(One of God's Shepherds)

The first time that I saw him
He was baptizing me
Long braids, long white robe
Long boots up to his knees
He seemed to have a divine spirit
That really captured me
He asked me do I accept
Jesus Christ as my savoir
And I said yes
What this man was all about
I didn't have to guess
It was expressed in his eyes
A ray of light
A spirit of strength
Kindness and gentleness
After baptism I heard him speak
He bared his soul sharing the word
And the whole Church body wept
He humbled himself before the congregation
Tears formed and slid down my cheek
It was quite a revelation
I know that this man
Was one more shepherd
Chosen to call in God's sheep

The Statue of Liberty

(September 11, 2001)

She felt there was danger lurking there
Close around but she didn't know where
She heard this strange noise
And she wondered why
As she stood and she watched
From her harbor high
Planes that torpedoed from the sky
Carrying people aboard about to die
Wreaking havoc, devastation
And horror upon her land
Targeting as many people as they can
The terrorist had come to invade her space
Her safe haven for all colors and race
Causing death and destruction
She couldn't possibly erase
She didn't understand
For this had never happened before
An attack upon America upon her shores?
Still she stood tall her torch held high
One tear maybe two fell from her eye
She vowed she would forever
Hold her throne
For she knew that America
Could hold its own and that she's protected
From dusk to dawn for Americans are united
Courageous, ready, wise, and strong

Heroes in Flight

(9/11)

I know it's a terrible thing
To realize you're about to die
With your plane being hijacked
By terrorists who are trained to fly
Terrorists who tell you
What they are about to do
And your mind flashes
To your loved ones
And everything that matters to you
Their plan was to crash
Into the biggest and tallest
Buildings around, instilling fear!
Sabotaging our minds!
Killing hundreds, maybe thousands
On the ground
But you know you can't let that happen
As long as you have breath and are
Still around a quick decision
Must act in a flash, gotta do what it takes
To detour this plane crash
You know there's no choice
And what you have to do
It's a sacrificial thing
And the sacrifice is you!

Flight 93

(9/11/2001)

We thank God
For the efforts of the people
On that ill-fated flight
Passengers and crew members
Who gave their lives
While diverting the terrorists
In their murderous attacks
For had they not fought them
It would have been a direct strike
For hundreds of innocent people
Unaware of the terrorist plight
"May God bless them"
Thwarting the hijackers
Was very brave
Family and friends can be proud
Of their heroic ways
And revel in the thought of
How many lives they saved

Angels in the Sky

Crew and passengers Flight of 93
They adorn the garment of angels
As they did their heroic deed
Sacrificing their lives
Planting their heroic seed
We thank them the people on Flight 93
For all the people they may have saved
The whole world wants you to know
We thank you for being so brave
They call them first citizen's heroes
Of the 21st century I call them
Angels in the sky
For they did a courageous thing
To make sure that no one else would die
When they were told what was going on
They didn't give up, they were reborn
Armed with the armor of the Lord while in the sky
Being adorn with the garment of angels as they
Blazed their way to glory to their heavenly home up high

September 11: A Story

It was eight fifty in the morning
And I had just gotten out of bed
There was breaking news on
My TV set and this is what it said
A plane had hit the World Trade Center
In New York City
And I thought to myself
Oh my God! What a pity! I started to cry
What a terrible accident for anyone
I didn't realize that terrorists had come
And that this plane crash was purposely done
No place to go, no place to escape
What a horrible sight, what a twist of fate
And then eighteen minutes later, another plane approached
Slammed into the second building
First and second coach I knew by now
Something was deadly wrong, two planes would never
Crash into the same building head-on
And then they announced that by now it's a fact
Planes had been hijacked and steered off their track
Headed for New York, Washington, DC, Camp David,
The Pentagon, places they wanted to strike
Kidnapping passengers, using them in the attack
Oh what a heinous, horrific crime
That these people so filled with hate
Launched against the citizens of these our United States
All innocent people who had made their way to work
Trying to make an honest living the way they do every day
Some being kidnapped and slaughtered by a plane in the sky
Some being trapped with no hope for the buildings were too high
It was said that people were told not to leave

No one was sure of what was going on—some were unaware that
The damage was so strong—people started to flee for their lives
The elevators were shut down, everyone headed for the stairwell
And were downward bound
Many people made it out some battered and some maimed
Others couldn't make it out and their bodies inflamed
Some held on to the ledge until the buildings became too hot
They could no longer hold on and their bodies dropped
Some ran out of windows in fear of the fire
Forgot where they were and fell through the sky
In another hour, tower one fell down
Spread like lava all over the ground
Five or six miles the debris and ash fell
Sent people running everywhere
Was this some kind of hell?
Yes many of us were put to sleep
It was a rude awakening and Americans wept
But through tragedy we affirmed what America is all about
The way we joined forces left no doubt
Our spirit of love and brotherhood commenced in flight
For we are strong we are united and together we will fight
To keep our freedom secure, our liberty, and protect our rights

Dedicated Protectors, Firemen

Troops of firemen performing their duties
Didn't want others to burn
Bravely rushed in to save them
And never returned
Only thinking of the others
As they made their way
Into the gates of heaven
On that very day

Spirit of Cooperation

(September 11, 2001)

The spirit of cooperation was ignited
In the wake of 9/11
When all broke loose
In the dawn with the rising sun
Early in the light of day
So many lives were blown away
In plane crashes New York's Twin Towers
All around! Hot lava all over the ground
Bodies were strewn all over town
Fiery concrete smoke hot steel
Ash smut and darkness everywhere
People running scrambling for safety
Trying to reach fresh air
Our soldiers our fireman paramedics
Policemen, U.S. citizens, people from all over
Suffering the same fate
The buildings were totaled
Reality seemed to have escaped
Terrorist trying to put us in bondage, in a life of fear
They didn't realize the family bonding
That Americans share here
For in war and troubled times we are a united front
We share One God One spirit One mind
We will together face aggressors to our Country
Of any kind
Everyone worked from dawn to dusk dusk to dawn
Sweating profusely digging for victims
Hoping to find someone trying to find people

Who were now buried treasure their since of anticipation
No cup could measure the ecstasy of joy each time
Someone was found alive swelled them up with relief
And spiritual pride For in times of war 911 emergencies
And devastations we stand side by side
In the spirit of cooperation
Helping each other throughout our nation

No Flag Like Our Flag!

(The American Flag, USA Stars and Stripes)

Our democracy has been strengthened
And our flags are flying high
We are uniting in our troubles
And for our freedom we will die
For terrorists cannot dictate to us
Or take away our rights
For we will take on any challenge
To preserve our way of life
No matter when no matter what our strife
For there is no flag like our flag
And we hold our banner high
We've fought many battles
And lost many lives
And earned its right to fly
We've lost our sons our daughters
Our moms and our dads
To people who thinks that a democracy is bad
From sea to shining sea in protection of
Our Civil Rights and liberty we will fight
With a united loyalty
In God we trust

About the Author

Bennie is a person full of unexplained
poetry, short stories, and wit.

CPSIA information can be obtained
at www.ICGtesting.com
Printed in the USA
BVHW080351020119
536773BV00010B/925/P